LIFE SKILLS

SURVIVING IN THE WILD

John Townsend

Heinemann

www.heinemannlibrary.co.uk Visit our website to find out more information about Heinemann Library books.	**To order:** ☎ Phone +44 (0) 1865 888066 Fax +44 (0) 1865 314091 Visit www.heinemannlibrary.co.uk

Heinemann Library is an imprint of Capstone Global Library Limited, a company incorporated in England and Wales having its registered office at 7 Pilgrim Street, London, EC4V 6LB – Registered company number: 6695582

Heinemann is a registered trademark of Pearson Education Limited, under licence to Capstone Global Library Limited

Text © Capstone Global Library Limited 2009
First published in hardback in 2009
Paperback edition first published in 2011

Edited by Pollyanna Poulter
Designed by Philippa Jenkins and Hart MacLeod
Original illustrations © Pearson Education Limited
  by Gary Slater
Picture research by Elizabeth Alexander and
  Maria Joannou
Production by Alison Parsons
Originated by Modern Age Repro House Ltd.
Printed and bound in China by South China
  Printing Company Ltd.

ISBN 978 0 431112 47 3 (hardback)
13 12 11 10 09
10 9 8 7 6 5 4 3 2 1

ISBN 978 0 431112 63 3 (paperback)
15 14 13 12 11
10 9 8 7 6 5 4 3 2 1

British Library Cataloguing-in-Publication Data
Townsend, John, 1955-
Surviving in the wild. - (Life skills)
796.
A full catalogue record for this book is available from the British Library.

Acknowledgements
We would like to thank the following for permission to reproduce photographs: © Alamy: pp. 19 (Christian Kosanetzky/Imagebroker), 21 (Suzy Bennett), 49 (Zefa RF/Stefan Schuetz); © Corbis: pp. 37 (Christine Mariner/Design Pics), 43 (Galen Rowell); © FLPA: pp. 17 (Michael & Patricia Fogden/Minden Pictures), 32 (Chris Newton), 33 top (Phil McLean); © Getty Images: pp. 25 (Visuals Unlimited), 35 (Photonica/Peter Hannert); © Istockphoto: p. 7; © PA Photos: p. 38 (AP/Lynn Hey); © Photolibrary: pp. 5 (Everton Macduff), 15 (Alaska Stock Images), 27 and 30 (Animals Animals/Earth Scenes), 29 (Phototake Inc); © Rex Features: pp. 22, 40 (Asgeir Helgestad/Nature Picture Library); © Science Photo Library: p. 33 bottom (Chris Hellier); © Werner Herzog Film: p. 47.

Cover photograph of boy crawling into tent reproduced with permission of © Corbis (B. Bird/zefa), and bear © Istockphoto (Daniel Kourey).

We would like to thank Mike Perrin and Jeff Randall for their invaluable help in the preparation of this book.

Every effort has been made to contact copyright holders of material reproduced in this book. Any omissions will be rectified in subsequent printings if notice is given to the Publishers.

Essex County Council Libraries

Contents

Some words are printed in bold, **like this**. You can find out
what they mean by looking in the glossary.

WILD PLACES

What would you do if you got stranded in a jungle? How would you cope if you got lost in a desert? Would you know what to do if you were the only survivor of a plane crash high in the mountains?

SKILLS TO SURVIVE

Believe it or not, some people have found themselves in situations just like these. Some have known what to do and survived to tell their stories. With a little skill, knowledge, and good sense, people can survive in some of the wildest places on Earth.

Another world

Most people live in towns and cities. Few of us spend much time far from "civilisation" with all its facilities, help, and services nearby. Long ago, our ancestors were hunters and gatherers in the great outdoors. Now, we probably wouldn't know how to look after ourselves out there – not without being able to phone for a pizza every so often!

Empty spaces

There are still many "wild places" left where people are few and far between. Nearly half Earth's land surface is classed as **wilderness**. This land is occupied by just 2.4 percent of the world's population. Wilderness provides some of the toughest places for humans to live on the planet.

Going wild

Some people like the idea of getting back to nature and escaping from the pressures of modern life. After all, there's an amazing world out there to explore. Many of us enjoy a sense of freedom by camping, hiking, canoeing, skiing, and horse riding in the great outdoors. But it's one thing to choose to live "in the wild" for a few days, it's quite another to find yourself suddenly stranded, with only your wits and skills to keep you alive.

Every year people get lost in deserts, mountains, forests, swamps, and remote places. No one deliberately sets off unprepared or expects to get lost, but weather conditions or medical emergencies can suddenly strike. That's when wilderness survival skills can make the difference between life and death.

By knowing something about the basic needs of food, shelter, and water – and by knowing key survival techniques – you'll be better able to survive in even the wildest of places until help arrives. So keep this book handy, just in case!

Would you know how to survive in the wild?

BEING PREPARED

Whether you're heading off on an expedition, or whether you just happen to find yourself stranded somewhere, a few essential items can make all the difference.

ESSENTIAL EQUIPMENT

A survival kit is important for any wilderness trip. Although the contents will vary according to climate and conditions, there are three absolute essentials any kit should contain. All of which need to be packed in a tough, waterproof container:

1. Fire-starting equipment
2. First aid items
3. Signalling items, such as a mirror and whistle.

Advice before setting off

Before heading out, inform someone about your route, destination, and when you expect to be back. After all, if you don't tell someone where you are going, no one will look for you if you get lost. Emergency services could possibly not even know that you are missing!

If rescue teams need to **track** a person or group it is much easier if they know a proposed route, so always keep someone informed of your plans. Be sure you call the person you informed when you return, or they may think you are missing when you are not!

• CHECKLIST •

The following things should always be packed in a survival kit:

- Lighter or waterproof matches
- A metal water container for boiling water
- Fishing line/hooks
- Candle
- Plastic bags
- Needle and thread
- Pocket-knife
- Torch
- Map and compass
- Food and water
- Mobile phone (this may not help you, but it is always best to take it)
- Water purification tablets or drops.

Just in case

Even if hikers don't plan to camp overnight in wild country, it is always wise to carry some sort of emergency "body shelter" in a rucksack. A plastic sheet can always be made into a makeshift tent if necessary. Ideally, it would be sensible to carry a sleeping bag, tube tent, and bin liners through rugged terrain, just in case the mist descends or the weather turns bad. In fact, sudden harsh weather conditions can turn a wilderness hike into a nightmare.

Hikers should always check weather forecasts before heading out cross-country (see page 53 for websites that give detailed forecasts days ahead). Even with such information, it pays to expect the unexpected – so always prepare for the worst and hope for the best!

Getting it Right

In Case of Emergency (ICE) is the idea that everyone should put an emergency contact name and number into their mobile phone under the headword "ICE". This, or an ICE card carried in a pocket, can give emergency services important information if a person is found injured and unable to talk.

Keep your kit packed together in an airtight, waterproof, crushproof can. You can use the can to boil water for your tea!

NAVIGATION

One of the keys to surviving in any wild place is knowing where you are and being able to find your way back. Anyone hiking should bring a good map (in a plastic cover) and have the skill to use it. Even so, every year people become lost and confused in some of the world's wildest areas.

Even experienced people can run into trouble and get lost – a map can get washed away, a compass can get damaged. What are the basic rules for anyone lost and alone in the wilderness? Simply remember one word: STOP.

People who continue to move when they find themselves lost and alone in the wilderness, always end up further away from where they should be.

If you decide, after waiting some days to be rescued, that no one is looking for you, you may have to try to find your own way to safety. Even without a map and compass, all is not lost!

• CHECKLIST •

S = STOP

Collect your thoughts and don't panic. Spend time looking around and assessing the scene.

T = THINK

Calmly weigh up the situation. Remaining positive is a real challenge but a key to survival.

O = OBSERVE

Note the weather, terrain, risks, and conditions. Spend time assessing your surroundings.

P = PLAN

Once you've come to terms with the situation, work out a clear plan. If you know people will come looking for you, stay where you are.

TIP

It is possible to navigate without a compass:

- **Where the Sun sets is west.**
- **At night, the North Star shows which direction north is.**
- **The Sun rises in the east. When it is light outside, it is often safe to begin moving again. But keep to one direction to avoid walking around in circles.**
- **If you see running water, follow it downstream. It can eventually lead to houses or people.**

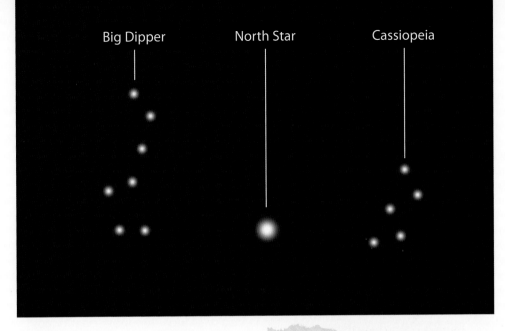

Big Dipper   North Star   Cassiopeia

The North Star is often the brightest star in the night sky and is located between the Big Dipper and Cassiopeia constellations.

Stop at night

In remote areas (unless you are in a desert) stop walking at least one hour before sunset, and always avoid travelling in unfamiliar areas after dark. You'll want to stop anyway, as it takes at least an hour to prepare for a night in the wilderness. Before making any preparations in the way of shelter, bedding, or fire, check through all equipment, laying everything out, and deciding how each item can be used to its best effect.

Getting it Right

If the Sun is shining, you can create a compass of your own to check on your general direction. Push a stick upright into the ground and note where its shadow ends. Wait about an hour before noting where it ends a second time. The line going between those two points should run approximately east to west. Another way to find north is to consult nearby trees and rocks. Moss usually grows more on the northern side of rocks and trees in the Northern Hemisphere, while spider webs tend to be on the south side of trees.

SAFE AND SOUND

There are four basic human needs for surviving in the wilderness. These are: warmth, sleep, water, and food. Without all four, anyone trying to live in open country can soon be at risk. The most important of these four needs varies depending on your specific circumstances.

Warmth

It is vital to maintain the correct body temperature as becoming too hot, or too cold, for too long is dangerous. In most wilderness survival situations the problem is how to stay warm. Even in deserts, where there is no shade from the burning Sun, temperatures drop rapidly during the night and it can become very cold.

Sleep

People need a certain amount of sleep to keep their body and mind working properly. Without proper sleep, our minds begin to fail and we cannot make sensible decisions. That is why a sheltered place to rest is a priority.

Water

The human body is about 60 percent water and therefore needs a constant supply of drinking water. The average person may survive for three days without water. However, it is important not to wait until supplies run dry before looking for more.

Food

On average it may be possible to survive for three weeks without eating. Whereas warmth and shelter are normally the first priority if someone gets lost in the wilderness, gathering food is usually next on the requirements list.

Shelter

Some kind of shelter is important, not just as a safe place to sleep, but also as protection from the Sun, insects, wind, rain, snow, heat or cold, and possibly wild animals. Survival experts sometimes warn that the most common mistake when making a shelter is to make it too large. A shelter must be large enough to protect but small enough to contain body heat, especially in the cold.

TIP

Avoid making a shelter beside rivers, water below the high-water mark, or anywhere at risk of flooding. This is a good way to avoid biting insects, too, as they often live by water! If in the mountains, avoid making a shelter near **avalanche** or rockslide areas, or in areas exposed to wind.

Getting it Right

Build a shelter by securing a long, strong stick to a tree at about waist height. Lay two more strong sticks on the floor on either side of the one secured to the tree. Lay a plastic sheet over the top stick, so the same amount of material is hanging on both sides. Tuck the material under the sticks on the floor, and spread it out inside to serve as flooring. If no plastic sheet is available, the roof will have to be made from branches and leaves.

A one-person shelter can easily be made using a plastic sheet, three sticks, and a tree.

Stick attached to tree

Plastic sheet

Ground sticks

FIRECRAFT

Once some kind of shelter is in place, think about lighting a fire. A good fire can meet many needs, not only warmth and comfort. As well as cooking and preserving food, it can also be used to purify water, sterilize bandages, signal for rescue, and provide protection from wild animals.

The first decision is where to make a fire. If it is very cold, you may be tempted to light a fire inside your shelter. Doing this would be extremely dangerous. Near to the shelter – just down-wind of it – is best. The fire should be protected, but not so near that it will fill your shelter with smoke and sparks!

WARNING!

Never light a fire without adult supervision (unless you are in an extreme survival situation). Every year, young people start forest fires accidentally.

*Using a hand drill is one of the simplest friction methods. Cut a V-shaped notch in a fireboard and place a piece of bark underneath it to catch the falling ember. Roll a **spindle** stick in the notch until it glows red and an ember forms.*

Spindle

Fireboard

Notch

Bark

Starting a fire

Any survival kit should include special waterproof matches with a striker pad (stored safely) in a waterproof container. Without them, things become much more difficult. It could even become necessary to use other methods to spark a flame, such as by directing bright sunshine through a lens (from binoculars, a camera, or a magnifying glass) onto a dry surface.

To do this, tilt the lens to concentrate the Sun's rays on the **tinder**. Hold the lens still until the tinder smoulders. Gently blow or fan the tinder to make a flame. Though this method is good it is not much use in fog!

If all else fails, you may have to try the friction method, which was used by people long ago (and is similar to that shown in the diagram opposite). They made sparks using friction caused by striking flints, or rubbing sticks, to ignite fine wood fibres.

Ablaze

For a good fire, you need three things: tinder, **kindling**, and fuel. Tinder is any dry material that ignites with a few sparks. **Charred** cloth is a useful tinder. You can make charred cloth in advance by heating cotton cloth until it turns black, but does not burn. When lighting a fire, you can use the cloth to keep a spark smouldering.

For kindling, use small, dry twigs that quickly ignite from the burning tinder. Tinder heats up fast and then needs

Getting it Right

One of the best designs for a campfire is a tepee shape, with the tinder and kindling in the centre and bigger logs propped up on the outside. This allows air to circulate well and – as the fire burns – the outside logs will dry out, if they are damp, fall inward, and feed the fire.

to be supported by fuel – the main material that takes longer to ignite but burns slowly and steadily.

Keeping fire safe

With the fire now alight, it's best to keep it burning all the time, so a constant supply of fuel is necessary. Work with others in your group to find more fuel. You could share out jobs and have a rota. The fire should never be left unattended, in case sparks blow near the shelter.

When it's time to move on, burn all rubbish and make sure the fire has gone out completely. Smouldering campfires, revived, and fanned by the wind, can destroy huge areas of wilderness.

WHATEVER THE WEATHER

Being out in the elements means being at the mercy of nature. Simple clues can warn if bad weather is on the way. This old saying can be a good clue as to the approaching weather:

> *"Red sky at night, shepherds' delight; red sky at morning, shepherds take warning."*
>
> Unknown

At dusk, a red sky indicates that the next day could be dry and fine. This is because the Sun is shining through dust particles that are being pushed ahead of a high-pressure system, bringing dry air. A red sky at dawn often means that an approaching, low-pressure system is bringing a lot of moisture in the air. This can mean a storm is on its way.

Lightning

Camping in thunder and lightning should be avoided at all costs if possible. It is also best to keep out of any wooded areas in a bad thunderstorm. The advice when caught in such a storm is to find shelter as soon as storm clouds start to gather and the thunder approaches.

Never stand under a tree – if lightning strikes, electricity will shoot down the trunk, through the roots, and into the ground, causing a powerful shock.

To work out how far away lightning is striking, count the seconds between the flash and the thunderclap. If it's less than five seconds, take shelter immediately. If possible, head for a building or vehicle. Otherwise, shelter in a hollow, such as a ditch or cave. Crouch, with your feet close together and your head down, to reduce your contact with the ground and the chance of being struck. It's usually safe to come out after there has been no thunder or lightning for 30 minutes.

TIP

A campfire can tell you what weather to expect. On a fine and clear day the smoke rises steadily. But if it starts swirling and descending, the air pressure is falling and you can expect bad weather.

Getting it
Right

Even when trying to survive in difficult conditions, it is important to respect the environment by keeping your campsite clean, tidy, and safe. Extinguish a campfire at least half an hour before leaving, by drizzling water over it. Before you go, hold your hands above it to check that it is no longer producing heat. If it is, pour on more water.

Anyone camping out in the open knows that the weather can be changeable.

Water And Food

You are in the middle of nowhere. You have built your shelter and fire – what comes next? Now it is time to think about food and drink.

DRINKING WATER

No one can survive for long without water. In hot areas, where you lose water rapidly through perspiration, water is especially vital for survival. Even in cold areas, a minimum of two litres (half a gallon) of water each day is needed. In a survival situation, finding an adequate water supply is one of your most urgent needs.

Finding water

Apart from in desert areas, water is often not far away. Places to look for water include cracks in rocks, cavities in plants or trees, and valley bottoms. Even if streams are dry, there may be water just below the surface.

Rainwater collected in clean containers, or from plants, is usually safe for drinking. However, water from lakes, ponds, swamps, springs, or streams may often contain bacteria and disease. You will need to use water purification tablets (follow the directions provided), or boil the water for about 10 minutes, to make sure it is safe to drink. Water melted from ice or snow also needs boiling to purify it.

Getting it Right

All plants contain moisture. When they **transpire**, they release tiny droplets from their leaves and stems. To collect these droplets of pure water, encase the living tips of a growing plant in a plastic bag. Secure the opening of the bag around the branch, stem, or trunk. Make sure the seal is as airtight as possible, that some of the plastic bag is lower than the airtight seal, and the bag can carry the weight of any collected water. After several hours, you could find you've collected a cup of safe, drinkable water – so long as the plant isn't poisonous!

DID YOU KNOW?

The water-holding frog lives in desert areas of Australia. After the rain, it swells up with water before burrowing underground where it stays until the next rainfall. When Native Australians are trying to survive in the desert, they sometimes find a few frogs to get a drink. By gently squeezing a water-holding frog, they get a lifesaving drink of "frog water". The frog is released unharmed – just a bit thirsty!

Collecting water

Heavy dew can provide enough water for a life-saving drink. Get yourself a cupful by tying rags, or tufts of fine grass, around your ankles and walking through damp grass before sunrise. The rags absorb the dew, which can then be wrung out into a container.

Sometimes, even in desert areas, it is possible to collect moisture overnight. Dig a hole and line it with a plastic sheet. By morning, there may be enough dew collected in the bottom to cool your throat!

WARNING!

Never drink seawater – a little will make you sick and a lot will kill you.

FINDING FOOD

Food survival kits should contain tinned and dried food as well as multi-vitamin pills, to ensure a well-balanced food supply. Anyone living in the wild for long periods will become weak or ill without a varied diet of **proteins**, fats, **carbohydrates**, vitamins, and minerals. Many of these **nutrients** can be found naturally in the wilderness in plants, insects, and animals. The skill is knowing how to find and prepare them.

Meat and fish provide a lot of the nutrients humans need, but hunting is not advisable unless you're an expert. However, gathering some sources of protein – such as bird's eggs – can be easier. Eggs can be boiled, baked, or fried and are a nutritious survival food.

WARNING!

You should never collect wild bird's eggs unless you are in a real life-or-death situation. Collecting bird's eggs is illegal.

Fishing

Most fish found in fresh water can be eaten, although some are more pleasant tasting than others. The best times to manage a catch are just before dawn or just after dusk. Hooks can be baited with insects, worms, small fruits, bread, or raw meat and left on lines overnight.

It is best to eat fish as soon after catching them as possible. To prepare a dead fish, cut off its head, tail, and fins and remove its innards. It's easier to remove the bones after the fish has been cooked. In fact, fish don't need a lot of cooking.

Ideally, fish are best wrapped in foil and left in hot ashes to cook. If no foil is handy, there are two other basic cooking methods that are useful in the wild: hot rock cooking and cooking in mud.

Hot rock cooking

Light a fire on a bed of stones. After about half an hour the rocks should be very hot. Brush away the fire and ashes, then cook food directly on the hot stones, which retain their heat. This survival cooking method is ideal for fish, thin meat slices, and frying eggs. It's much like a barbecue.

Cooking in mud

Wrap meat in fresh grass and tie it up in a bundle, completely covering the meat. Cover the package in about 3 cm (1 in.) of wet clay or mud, with no grass showing through. Place the package on a deep bed of embers and build a fire above it.

A good-sized fish takes about an hour to cook while a small animal, such as a rabbit, takes about four hours. Always overcook food in the wild to make sure it is safe to eat. *Bon appetit!*

 Fish can be boiled, grilled, or fried depending on the equipment available.

Don't try this at home!

Desperate situations may require desperate eating. Sometimes the only way to obtain important nutrients in the wilderness is to eat edible bugs. However disgusting it may seem, grubs, worms, and insects are an excellent food supply for survival.

Insects live almost everywhere on the planet, often in large numbers. They can be easy to catch in rotten logs, under the bark of dead trees, on plants, in soil – anywhere that's moist and shady.

Flying insects are best caught at night by hanging thin cloth in front of a light, over a bowl of water. The insects attracted to the light will fly into the cloth and drop into the water. Once the wings are removed, these can be roasted for a rich source of protein.

• CHECKLIST •

The following edible bugs are likely to be found in a forest **habitat**.

1. Insect **larvae** (grubs) are easy to find in cool, damp places under rocks, in rotting bark, and in the ground. Grubs are safe to eat raw, but are usually preferred cooked.

2. Grasshoppers can often be heard "chirping" in long grass but can be hard to catch – a cool morning is the best time. Grasshoppers should be cooked because they carry **parasites**.

3. Ants and termites can be found in many habitats. Their nests are generally in the ground. To collect ants, disturb a nest with a stick, allow the ants to climb the stick, and dip the stick into a container of water to remove them. Ants can be safely eaten raw or cooked but be careful they don't bite back!

4. Slugs and snails can be found in damp areas under rocks and logs. Some slugs are quite big so it can be easy to collect a full meal. Although they can be eaten raw, they are slimy and are probably better cooked.

5. Maggots, which are the larvae of flies, can often be found on decaying material. They are safe to eat raw or cooked.

6. Earthworms can usually be dug out of moist, warm soil. They can be eaten raw or cooked.

For native Australians, the witchetty grub was eaten when food was scarce. It has since become something of a delicacy with some Australians and even tourists.

CAN YOU BELIEVE IT?

A famous survival story made world news in 1972 when a plane crashed in the Andes Mountains in South America. Of the 45 people on the plane, 25 survived the crash itself. But they were high up in freezing mountains, with no cold-weather clothing or footwear suitable for the ice and snow.

The survivors only had a small amount of food: chocolate bars, snacks, and a few bottles of wine. They managed to melt snow on strips of metal taken from the plane seats and left in the Sun. The water was then dripped into empty wine bottles. Even with strict rationing, their food soon began to run out. There were no plants or animals on the snow-covered mountain. The survivors were so starving that they felt forced to eat their dead companions.

"We tried to eat strips of leather torn from luggage. We ripped open seat cushions hoping to find straw, but found only inedible foam. Again and again I came to the same conclusion: unless we wanted to eat the clothes we were wearing, there was nothing here but aluminium, plastic, ice, and rock."

Nando Parrado, survivor

Eventually, after 72 days, 14 survivors got down the mountain alive.

QUIZ

COPING IN THE WILDERNESS

1) **If you were going hiking with friends, what preparations would you make?**
   a) Ensure each person carries a survival kit as well as proper outdoor equipment.
   b) Tell the police, mountain rescue service, and the army all your plans.
   c) Just head off to enjoy a good time in the fresh air and not worry about problems until they happen.

2) **If you were lost all by yourself in a large forest, what would you do?**
   a) Spend time assessing your situation, your likely location, and the best direction you should take.
   b) Climb up a tree, with a red rag, to wave at any helicopters.
   c) Keep walking in any direction as you're bound to find a road eventually.

3) **If you needed to make a shelter in the wilderness, what would you do?**
   a) Find a sheltered spot where you can keep safe and light a fire.
   b) Build a little house on a hill with a view of the sunset.
   c) Find a large tree to camp under so you've got plenty of wood for a great campfire.

4) **If you were in the wilderness and ran out of water, what would you do?**
   a) Tie small plastic bags over plants to collect their water vapour.
   b) Dig as many holes as you can and try to find some frogs.
   c) Drink water out of dirty rivers and streams.

5) **If you needed to find food in the wilderness, what would you do?**
   a) Try fishing in a nearby stream with baited hooks on lines.
   b) Make a spear and head off into the forest to kill a few deer.
   c) Use your mobile phone to call for a take-away.

6) **You've got nothing to eat and find an ants' nest, what do you do?**
   a) Poke a stick in it, shake the ants off into water, and eat them.
   b) Stamp on the nest to kill all the ant grubs.
   c) Build a fire over the nest, light it, and cook the ants until they're crisp, crunchy, and golden.

See page 50 to find out what kind of survivor you are!

Dangers In The Wild

Knowing what you can and can't eat safely is one of the keys to surviving in the wild. Many plants are **toxic** and one small mistake can be deadly. Anyone planning to go on a wilderness expedition should learn, in advance, how to identify plants that are best left well alone.

DO YOUR RESEARCH

Although some plants growing in the wild are nutritious, the rule should always be "if in doubt, don't touch". Before you go, learn about plants that are native to where you are going. You can even get guide books with clear pictures that will help you to identify hundreds of wild plants, safe or not.

Poison Ivy

One plant that should always be avoided is the woody vine, Poison Ivy. This can be a problem because it grows in different forms, with different leaf shapes, and other plants in the same habitat look like it.

Anyone exploring the woods and fields of the Great Plains in the United States might come across Poison Ivy. It is found coast-to-coast, from southern Canada to Mexico, as well as in the West Indies and China. Other varieties are Poison Oak, Poison Sumac, and the Florida Poison Tree. The plants contain a chemical that can give people an itchy rash, blisters, and a nasty **allergic** reaction. So don't touch them!

TIP

In 2007, a Scottish teenager had to survive alone for two nights in an Australian rainforest after he became lost while hiking. He used some of the techniques he had seen on a television bushcraft programme. William Bliss, aged 19, ate wild watercress and kept warm using bracken fronds while he waited to be rescued in Otway Ranges National Park, Victoria, south Australia. Just a little knowledge helped him survive in the wild.

Plant patrol

Wherever you happen to be in the wild, there are bound to be plants that can harm the skin and eyes, and others that are very toxic. Just one bite of some roots, pods, leaves, fruit, or fungi can be **fatal**.

This pure white mushroom is called the Destroying Angel, and it could kill anyone who eats it. It also looks like some edible species, so it is always best to stay away from any totally white mushrooms.

Getting it Right

Always stay away from any wild or unknown plants if they have:

- Beans, bulbs, or seeds inside pods
- Milky sap
- Spines, fine hairs, or thorns
- Leaves and an "almond" scent in places
- Grain heads with pink, purple, or black spurs
- Brightly coloured parts, such as berries.

If you do ever have to collect wild plants for food, always remember:

- Never eat edible plants if they are growing in dirty or contaminated water
- Never eat wild mushroom fungi
- Never eat edible fruit that is starting to spoil, or shows signs of mildew or fungus.

DANGEROUS ANIMALS

Most animals in wild places will keep well out of sight. Even though they are likely to be watching you, animals are usually the last things to worry about in the wild, as they are the ones in greatest danger.

If you happen to be in an area where large **predators** live, just a little common sense will prevent a scary encounter. Be wary of any animals, including large grazing animals with horns and hooves, particularly when they are protecting their young. Always move carefully through their environment and respect wildlife.

The other golden rule is to never leave food lying around your camp, as this is bound to attract some unwelcome animals. Every year, campers wake up to find their tents being raided by all kinds of creatures, from alligators to big cats, and even polar bears! Very often, people who get attacked by such animals have only themselves to blame. A bit more care and research could prevent any dangerous encounters.

Boar country

Wild boars live in the forests of northern Europe – including parts of the UK – and have been introduced to New Zealand and the United States. They are shy animals and, if left alone, are unlikely to attack people.

Remember these rules when hiking in an area where wild boar live:

1. If you see wild boar, do not approach them. Try to leave the area by the same route you arrived.

2. All dogs should be kept on a lead if walking them in countryside where boar live.

3. If you see wild boar and you have a dog off the lead, call the dog and put it on the lead immediately. If the dog chases wild boar, stay at a safe distance and call the dog back. Do not approach the boar.

4. Sows with young piglets are likely to be more dangerous than other boar as they may defend their young. Therefore, dense woodland should be avoided, as these areas are often used as resting and breeding sites.

5. If you can see boar that are a safe distance away, it may be possible to wait until they have left before moving on.

TIP

If a bear lunges right at you, drop to the ground, lie face down, and clasp your hands behind your neck. Never run away – running may trigger a chase response in the bear.

Bear country

The breathtaking US national parks of Yosemite in California, and Yellowstone in Wyoming, hold something besides amazing scenery that may take your breath away. Yosemite is home to black bears, while Yellowstone is home to both grizzly and black bears. Sometimes campers meet them face-to-face!

You can avoid bumping into a bear on a hiking trail by:

1. Being noisy – occasional shouts or singing will lessen the chances of a sudden bear encounter.

*A black bear will be attracted to any tent with even small scraps of food inside. To avoid unwelcome visitors in your tent, store food in an airtight, **bear-proof container**, and leave well away from your tent.*

2. Hiking in groups and taking extra care where vision might be obstructed by trees.

3. Never hiking after dark – bears seem to be more active on trails at dusk and dawn.

4. Avoiding any dead animals – bears often defend this source of food.

HIDDEN RISKS

Large, wild animals only pose a small risk in some wilderness areas. Often, the bigger risk is from smaller creatures. In fact, many are so small or well **camouflaged** that it's hard to see them at all. Small creatures that pose threats to humans include:

- mosquitoes,
- arachnids, such as spiders, scorpions, and ticks,
- leeches, which are not dangerous as such but the area of skin they suck onto can become infected,
- poisonous snakes or lizards,
- dangerous fish, such as piranha, electric eels, or stingrays.

Mosquitoes

The deadliest creature on earth is the *anopheles* mosquito. Mosquitoes cause more than 500 million cases of **malaria**, and one to three million deaths, each year. The 3,000 species of mosquito, including 200 in North America, do not all carry the same diseases, but you don't want to run the risk of being bitten by any. You can reduce the risk of being bitten by wearing repellent, long sleeves, and sleeping under a mosquito net. Avoid sleeping near water, or leaving water nearby in open containers, as this will attract them.

Ticks

There are about 850 species of tick in forests and grasslands around the world. You probably won't even feel a tick as it hops onto your body, pokes its head through your skin, and has a drink of your blood. If you find a tick in your skin, remove it as soon as possible but be careful as this can be tricky and dangerous. Check if its mouth is already under your skin. You will need to use special rotating tweezers (which can be found at a pharmacy). If red spots appear, even after a few weeks, consult a doctor.

Scorpions

There are about 1,200 species of scorpion in the world, but only around 20 can be dangerous to humans. Even then, most deaths resulting from scorpion stings are in babies, the elderly, or from a major allergic reaction. A sting is painful, causes swelling, muscle spasms, numbness, and tingling. The pain usually goes within an hour and all symptoms should be gone in 24 hours. Medical help is only needed if bad reactions persist.

Avoid stings by shaking clothes before getting dressed (a good rule of thumb for removing all creepy-crawlies), and checking inside shoes before putting them on. Also check under bedding before getting inside.

Arachnids

Very few spiders are harmful to humans. But to anyone in the forest regions of the east coast of Australia – from Tasmania to north Queensland – look out! This is the habitat of the large, brown funnel-web spider. As its name suggests, this spider lives in a web with an opening shaped like a funnel. Put simply, this creature does not like being disturbed. If it bites, its venom gets into the blood stream and can cause a serious reaction.

The best way to stop venom spreading through the body is to tie a pressure bandage above the bite – tightly binding the entire limb. The patient should be kept still and taken for immediate medical help to be given **antivenom**.

Ticks are very small and unlikely to be seen as they wait for a warm-blooded animal to hop on to.

Snakes

If you're out in snake country, follow a few simple rules to reduce the chance of accidental snakebite:

1. Wear a good pair of snake-proof boots if you're going to be in snake country – and carry a stick.

2. Don't sleep next to bushes, tall grass, large boulders, or trees – they provide hiding places for snakes. Use mosquito netting and ensure it's tucked well under your sleeping bag.

3. Don't put your hands into dark places, such as rock crevices or hollow logs. You never know what may be hiding inside.

4. Don't step over logs. Instead, step on the log and look to see if there's a snake resting on the other side.

5. Avoid walking through heavy brush or tall grass and always look where you are walking.

6. Don't pick up any snake – even if you think it's harmless or dead.

Getting it Right

If you get bitten by a snake:

- Don't move around too much – try to be carried to help.

- Don't apply cold compresses to the bite.

- Don't cut into the bite with a knife or razor.

- Don't try to suck out the venom by mouth.

- Don't raise the site of the bite above the level of the heart.

Most snakes will usually try to get away from a human hiking through the undergrowth, but sometimes, as they bask in the Sun, they are taken by surprise and may bite in defence.

KEEPING OUT OF DANGER

1) What should you remember about eating wild plants?
a) They are quite delicious, especially with chocolate sauce.
b) It is risky, as many are toxic.
c) It is a cheap and good way to save money in the wild.

2) What should you do if you come across a bear in the wild?
a) Poke it with a stick and give it a cuddle.
b) Stand very still and try to back away quietly.
c) Take a photo so you can try to sell it for a great price.

3) If a bear lunges right at you, what should you do?
a) Find some honey to distract it.
b) Drop to the ground, lie face down, and clasp your hands behind your neck.
c) Hold on to your wallet.

4) If a funnel-web spider bites you, what should you do?
a) Jump around energetically to sweat out all the poison from your body.
b) Tie a tight bandage above the bite to stop the poison spreading, and get medical help.
c) Catch the spider to sell for its highly-valued venom.

5) If you find a tick on your body, what should you do?
a) Sprinkle it with salt and pepper until it drops off.
b) Use special tweezers to carefully twist it off.
b) Go to the police and sue the landowner where you got the tick.

6) If you're walking in snake country, what should you do?
a) Run around in bare feet coated with strong mustard.
b) Watch carefully in heavy brush, looking down all the time, and using a stick in tall grass.
b) Wear cheap, thigh-length boots.

See page 50 to find out if you'd successfully keep danger at bay!

Lifesavers

Stories of people being lost or stranded in wild places often tell of little things that save their lives. Maybe something they find in the wilderness helps them, or a simple thing ends up making the difference between life and death when things go wrong.

Friendly Plants

Despite some of the dangers that plants can pose, some wild vegetation can be of great help when trying to survive with very little.

Dandelion is a plant common to many parts of the world. Although often thought of as a garden weed, the leaves are safe to eat (raw or cooked). They are also a good source of nutrition and contain a range of vitamins, minerals, and protein. So if you're ever stuck in the middle of a forest with no food, a dandelion could be a useful friend!

Dock leaves are another common woodland plant. Many people know these are useful for rubbing on nettle rash stings to ease the discomfort. But, did you know, they can also be eaten? Curled dock is a widespread, edible species. It can be found in Europe and Asia, and has spread through North America and parts of Australia.

Both dock and dandelion leaves can taste bitter so may need to be boiled before being eaten.

Dock leaves can be used as a wild vegetable and are also an excellent source of both vitamin A and protein.

DID YOU KNOW?

In 2007, two Frenchmen, aged 34, survived seven weeks lost in the Amazon jungle by eating spiders, frogs, centipedes, and turtles. With only a compass, map, and 12 days of food, they had planned to trek 96 kilometres (60 miles) but got lost. They built a shelter and stayed put for three weeks. They lit fires, but no rescue came.

"I was so hungry I even had a go at the turtle's shell," said one of the Frenchmen, infested with worms that had burrowed into his flesh. He could hardly move after swallowing venom from a poorly cooked giant spider, and was covered with fleabites. Doctors said without proper nutrition he would have died within three days. His friend eventually staggered from the jungle to raise the alarm.

*Garlic or onion juice makes a good insect repellent, as well as an **antiseptic** that can be dabbed on minor wounds, such as cuts, sores, and rashes.*

Even in hot, dry areas, where few plants grow, people have survived by finding palm trees that provide both shade and coconuts. "Milk" from coconuts has a high water content but – be warned – it can also act as a laxative!

FIRST AID

For any group planning to stay outdoors, far from medical facilities, at least one person should be a qualified first aider with a full first aid kit. That way, most minor injuries and emergencies can be dealt with. Sometimes though, it's necessary to **improvise** when treating injuries.

For injuries such as bad cuts and open wounds, the first priority is to stop any bleeding by bandaging firmly. Bandages can be made quickly by tearing strips of fabric. Once the bleeding stops, clean the wound to prevent infection. To clean the skin around a wound, rinse (don't scrub) with a lot of water. For example, by holding it in the running water of a clean stream.

Even with regular cleaning and fresh bandages, some degree of infection is likely in a survival situation. As long as a wound can drain, it generally won't become life-threatening, despite how unpleasant it looks or smells.

Keeping warm and clean

A danger for anyone stranded in the cold is injury caused by frostbite – frozen body tissue. Light frostbite affects the skin, but if it gets into muscle, limbs freeze. Hands, feet, and the face are particularly vulnerable. If in a group, help prevent frostbite by using the "buddy system" – checking each other's faces often. If alone, cover your nose and the lower part of your face. Never try to thaw frostbite close to an open flame. Instead, gently rub the skin in lukewarm water.

DID YOU KNOW?

If no **antibiotics** are available and wounds become badly infected, there is one last resort: maggots! Maggots are great little workers. They can clean up the most infected of wounds because they feed on rotting body tissue. Within a few days, they can get rid of a nasty infection. So, to begin with, it's just a matter of letting flies get to the wound and then checking daily for maggots. When they appear, keep the wound covered, but keep checking it. As soon as all the bad tissue has gone, flush out the wound with clean water and wash out all the maggots. Then, just bandage the wound and it should heal normally.

Water works

Water is vitally important – not just for drinking and cleaning wounds. Washing with clean, sterile water can keep various infections, skin irritations, and even fleas at bay. However desperate the situation, wash hands, hair, and clothes whenever possible – and don't forget to look after your teeth.

With no toothbrush, you can use a chewing stick. Find a twig, chew one end to separate the fibres, and use this to brush your teeth. You could also wrap a clean strip of cloth around your finger and rub your teeth to wipe away food particles. Small amounts of sand, salt, or soap can also be used. It may not be as good as toothpaste, but it's better than nothing!

A good first aid kit in a waterproof bag doesn't take up much room in a rucksack, and could prove a lifesaver.

SIGNALS

Being able to signal for help could be a lifesaver in a survival situation. If you ever find yourself lost and alone in the wilderness, signalling for rescue is going to be one of your priorities. But how is it possible for someone to attract attention when rescuers are likely to be miles away?

In some situations, it might just be possible to send radio signals. So it's useful to know the most recent international, **phonetic**, English alphabet. This can be important when spelling out information on a crackly radio or phone line (see below).

Letters and their code words:

A	Alpha	**N**	November
B	Bravo	**O**	Oscar
C	Charlie	**P**	Papa
D	Delta	**Q**	Quebec
E	Echo	**R**	Romeo
F	Foxtrot	**S**	Sierra
G	Golf	**T**	Tango
H	Hotel	**U**	Uniform
I	India	**V**	Victor
J	Juliet	**W**	Whiskey
K	Kilo	**X**	X-Ray
L	Lima	**Y**	Yankee
M	Mike	**Z**	Zulu

Being seen

A stranded survivor is more likely to use visual signals to attract rescuers. That could mean using fire, smoke, a mirror, torch, flares, or markers.

The best place to signal from would be close to your shelter or a place with good visibility, such as a hilltop, clearing, or beach. A fire is by far the best way to signal, as it can be easily seen at night. Burning leaves and grass in the day will make plenty of smoke that can be seen for miles. Building three fires – in a straight line or triangle shape – is even better, as this is an internationally recognised distress signal. Remember to make sure that any fire you do build is controlled, and doesn't get out of hand and spread.

As well as fire, on a sunny day, a mirror – or anything shiny – is a great signalling tool. A polished cup, knife, glass, buckle, or tin can will all reflect the Sun's rays to any passing ship or plane. Flashing the SOS signal (see opposite) at a pilot has saved many a **marooned** survivor.

Spreading clothes on the ground or in a tree is another way to signal, particularly if they're white or brightly coloured. Arrange them in a large pattern to make them more likely to attract attention, or make a large flag that flaps in the wind.

DID YOU KNOW?

The three letters, SOS, are known throughout the world as a distress signal. The SOS signal can be transmitted visually or audibly. The visual code for SOS is: three short, three long, and three short signals; pause; repeat the signal. Audibly, that's: dot dot dot; dash dash dash; dot dot dot. An SOS ground to air signal can also be made by spelling out SOS in large letters, in an open space, using rocks and logs, or whatever is available. At night you can use a flashing light to signal the SOS code to an aircraft.

SOS simply means "HELP!".
Some believe it is an abbreviation
of "Save Our Souls".

LOST AND FOUND

Now and again, young people go missing in wild places.

In 2007, 12-year-old Michael Auberry got homesick when on a scout camp in the mountains of North Carolina, US. He decided to set off home but soon became lost. Michael's Scout Master, Dean Stinson, teaches his troops various life skills, which is just as well, as Michael needed plenty of them to survive alone.

When Michael realized he didn't know where he was, he did the right thing by stopping and waiting for someone to find him. A search party set out and eventually the park rangers rescued him. They praised his survival training and warm clothing for seeing him through. Michael survived three nights in temperatures below freezing. He took cover under branches and rocks, and drank creek water when the food he had ran out.

"Four days is a long time because he's so young" said 16-year-old co-scout, Zachary Miller. A friend of Michael's also gave some top advice:

Search teams are trained to find people lost in extreme conditions. Let's hope you never need one.

"We learned to stay put. You don't want to wander any farther than you should and you must use what you can around you to make a shelter, then collect food or water."
Friend of Michael Auberry

SURVIVAL OF THE FITTEST

1) Why is wild garlic a great plant to find when camping?
a) You can make its leaves into thread for knitting a blanket.
b) It adds a nice flavour to stews, but you'll need a good mouthwash the next day.
c) Its juice makes a good insect repellent and a useful antiseptic.

2) On a desert island, why could your life be saved by a palm tree?
a) You could chop it down to make a canoe to escape with.
b) You could climb up it to escape from rats.
c) You could drink from it, as well as get shade and shelter from its branches.

3) If you have to give first aid to someone with a bleeding wound, what should you do?
a) Act like a doctor and stay cheerful as you try to comfort them.
b) Insist that everyone is quiet and spotless before giving a blood transfusion.
c) Clean the wound with water and then bandage it to stop the bleeding.

4) What can you use to clean your teeth if you have no toothbrush?
a) Maggots.
b) A rag soaked in salty water rubbed over the gums every hour.
c) A twig with a chewed end that can be brushed between the teeth to remove food.

5) Using the phonetic alphabet, how do you spell out SOS?
a) Sausages On Sticks.
b) Save Our Souls.
c) Sierra Oscar Sierra.

6) If you see a helicopter on the horizon, how should you signal to it that you need help?
a) Take off your clothes, climb a tree, and wave them in the air.
b) Fire a rescue flare at the pilot and blow a whistle.
c) Get three fires to make smoke, flash sunlight with a mirror, and mark the ground with clothes.

See page 50 to find out how well you would cope in the wild!

Hostile Places

There's a good reason why so few people live in wilderness areas. It can be tough out there! Often the soil is thin, the ground is rocky, and it's difficult for plants to grow. On top of all that, the weather can be more than just hostile – it's often extreme.

Ice and Snow

Some of the most beautiful places on Earth are also the coldest. Areas with huge sculptures of ice, vast stretches of dazzling snow, and great glinting glaciers can be breathtaking. That's why some people brave the cold to experience such an extreme environment. But you'll need good survival skills to stay long in such icy surroundings.

There is very little insulating fat in the head, neck, wrists, and ankles so keep those areas warm and dry.

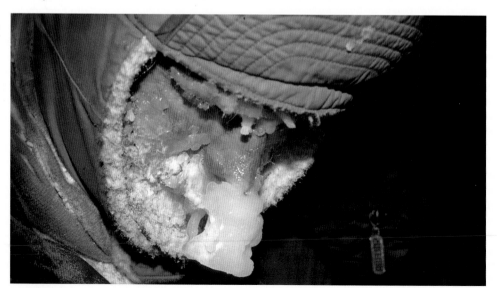

Closer to home

Millions of people around the world live in areas with extremely cold winters. For millions of others, a sudden freeze or heavy snowfall can happen from time to time. In such places, drivers should carry a few extras in their cars, to be on the safe side. After all, drivers and passengers often forget to wrap up warm when getting inside a car, because it has a heater. If the car was then to break down in freezing temperatures, everyone inside would be on their way to getting **hypothermia**.

If you live in a place where fiercely cold winters or snowstorms are likely to occur, make sure the car owner in your home is suitably prepared. Just in case of getting stuck in a snowstorm in a car, it always pays to carry blankets, torches, chocolate bars, and a shovel. A bottle of water is also a good idea. Even if it freezes, some drops can be thawed to drink if you get stranded. If you do get stranded, stay with the car. Rescuers are more likely to find you if you are inside it – especially if you spell out SOS nearby in the snow.

Getting it Right

Try remembering these four basic rules for surviving in extreme cold:

C Keep COVERED. That means all over, especially the top of your head.

O Avoid OVERHEATING. When you get too hot, you sweat, and your clothing absorbs the moisture. Dampness lessens the insulation of clothing and sweat cools the body.

L Wear your clothing LOOSE and in LAYERS. Wearing tight clothing restricts blood circulation and reduces the amount of insulating air trapped between the layers. Several layers of lightweight clothing are better than one thick layer, because the layers have warm air between them.

D Keep clothing DRY. Outer clothing should be waterproof – if not, it can become wet from snow melted by body heat.

MOUNTAIN SURVIVAL

Many mountain ranges have snow on their peaks through much of the year. Even in summer, the **summits** get very cold at night. Often, people who walk or ski in mountains go up in warm sunshine and don't realise how dangerous the higher slopes can become at night. As in all wilderness areas, the rule is: be prepared.

Danger on the slopes

With so many people heading up mountains each winter to ski, it's surprising so few ever need rescuing. That's probably because most people obey the rules: NEVER ski or walk alone on mountains, or go off the main ski slopes – that's where avalanches may strike.

Avalanche accidents rarely happen in ski areas, because workers control avalanche hazards with explosives. Even so, it pays to know about avalanche survival just in case. Some people think they'll be able to ski fast enough to escape an avalanche, but that is very unlikely.

DID YOU KNOW?

Twenty-seven-year-old mountain climber, Aron Ralston, made world news in 2003 with his famous survival story. When alone in the mountains of Utah, US, a boulder fell on him, trapping his arm. For six days he struggled to free himself while suffering from **dehydration** and hypothermia. Facing certain death, Ralston made the grim decision to snap his own bones and cut off his arm below the elbow, using a penknife. Once free, he staggered down the mountain to find help. He lived to tell the tale.

"I didn't have any sensation in my right hand from the time of the accident onward. When I amputated, I felt every bit of it. It hurt to break the bone, and it certainly hurt to cut the nerve. I agree with the people who say to never go out alone without telling someone where you are going. Normally, I do that. I didn't this time, because I miscalculated the risks."
Aron Ralston, survivor

Getting it **Right**

If caught in an avalanche:

- Seek shelter behind rocks, trees, or vehicles
- Crouch low, and turn away from the avalanche
- Cover your nose and mouth
- Brace against the impact, by holding onto something sturdy, like a tree
- Do not cry out or open your mouth as the avalanche is occurring.

As the avalanche slows:

- Pull your hands and arms to your face to make an air space
- Thrust and kick yourself to the surface, just before the snow comes to a complete stop
- Try to stay on the surface of the snow and work your way to the side of the avalanche
- Thrust an arm or ski pole towards the surface.

When the avalanche has stopped:

- Try to dig yourself out
- Always carry a whistle – blow it to attract attention.

If you do go for help, mark the route so a rescue party can follow it back to find others.

DESERTS

One of the most hostile environments on Earth is desert. Covering around a third of Earth's land surface, deserts are also the driest habitats in the world. Some desert areas receive less than 10 cm (4 in.) of rain each year. So it's hardly surprising that of what little rain falls, most of it quickly runs off the dusty surface or soon evaporates. It's hard to imagine anything being able to survive here, where air temperature can rise as high as 60°C (140°F) during the day.

Intense sunlight and heat dramatically increase the body's need for water. To conserve body fluids and energy, anyone crossing a desert will need a shelter during the day and should travel only at night.

Make your shelter at dusk or dawn and not in the full heat of the day.

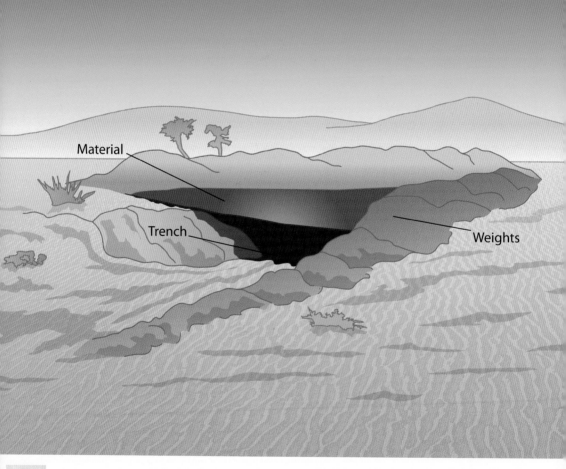

Material

Trench

Weights

Getting it Right

In a sandy area, you could make a shelter by digging a large trench and surrounding it with a mound on three sides (as shown opposite). Stretch material (a sheet of canvas is ideal) over the trench, weighing the edges down with sand or rocks. Inside, you will be much cooler and protected from sandstorms.

The Australian outback

Most of the deserts of Australia lie in the central and north-western part of the country. Each year, people get lost or need to be rescued from this harsh environment. That's often because they set off in a vehicle that breaks down.

Intense heat can overheat engines and also cause radios to fail. Mobile phones cannot be relied upon either, as they may not receive a signal in remote areas. Many people also underestimate the amount of water they need in the outback. People should take four to five litres (about two gallons) of water per person per day, as well as an extra three days' water and food on top of that – in case there truly is an emergency.

Another thing the police stress strongly: take an **EPIRB** (Emergency Position Indicating Radio Beacon), which is a personal distress beacon. These were once used mostly at sea, but now motorists can rent them to take across the outback. Such a device would surely have helped the American tourist who, in 1999, was rescued after wandering the Great Sandy Desert for 42 days!

RAINFOREST

Thick rainforests of hanging vines, thick roots, and swamps cover around six percent of Earth's total land surface. Life thrives in this wild place, and rainforests are home to up to 75 percent of all known plant and animal species – many of which are insects. Heavy rain falls many days of the year in a rainforest. This, along with the often warm temperatures, creates a humid climate.

Nasty nibblers

How do humans survive in hot, damp, and hostile rainforests? One of the biggest problems for people here is insects that bite. The smells of human sweat, breath, and body heat signal to mosquitoes that blood is there for drinking. Bites cannot only become infected and sore, but can spread dangerous tropical diseases.

Tropical treats

In the tropics, even the smallest scratch can quickly become infected because bacteria thrive there. Any wound needs treating promptly, with antiseptic cream and bandages, to stop insects biting further or laying eggs in the open flesh.

Getting it Right

The best way to get out of a dense rainforest is to find water and follow it downstream because people live near water. Move slowly and steadily, using a stick to part the vegetation in your path. Using a stick helps dislodge biting ants, spiders, or snakes. Never grasp at vines when climbing slopes, as they may have spines or sharp thorns.

Many years after the crash, Juliane returned to the wreck in the rainforest, to make a film about her amazing story of survival.

DID YOU KNOW?

In 1971, 17-year-old Juliane Koepcke was in a plane flying over the Amazon, in South America. Suddenly, the plane ran into a terrible storm and exploded. Juliane felt herself fly through the air, still strapped to her seat. She awoke three hours later, still strapped to her seat, in the mud, in the middle of the rainforest. Amazingly, she had only broken her collarbone, gashed her right arm, and lost vision in one eye. She was stunned, but remembered her father's advice about heading downhill in the jungle as it leads to water, and water leads to civilization. So Juliane set off, pushing her way through the forest.

After 10 days of walking and eating very little, Juliane came across a hunter's hut. There was salt and petrol inside, and she used these to clean her skin, which was full of grubs, hatching from eggs laid on her body by flies. The next day, some hunters arrived who took her to the nearest town for medical help. She made a full recovery. No one could believe a young girl in a torn miniskirt and one sandal could survive 10 days alone in the rainforest, and walk out alive.

One of the keys to her survival was her state of mind and utter determination. Positive thinking can be the secret to survival.

BUSHCRAFT

As we have seen, even in the most hostile places on Earth, it's still possible for humans to survive in the very worst circumstances. Some of the reports, about people surviving for long periods when stranded in the wildest environments, are truly amazing. In most cases, their success is down to a little knowledge and skill, some life-saving equipment, and the grim determination to keep going.

Yet not all wilderness experiences are quite so dramatic and dangerous. Many people want the challenge of living by their wits, sharing camp life, and experiencing nature close-up. So, they go and try it.

Terrestrial training

Numerous training courses and TV programmes have made wilderness skills popular today. The collection of survival techniques they explore – including firecraft, tracking, foraging, hunting, shelter building, using hand-made tools and natural materials – are together known as bushcraft.

Back to the wild

Learning bushcraft as a skill is becoming ever more popular. But what does all this recent interest tell us? It is probably that we are fascinated with pitching people against nature.

Despite most of us being familiar with a modern and sophisticated, urban way of life, it appears we still have a bit of hunter-gatherer in us. Maybe we also still want to be prepared should we ever end up living in caves again, like our ancient ancestors did all those years ago! Or perhaps it all comes back to our underlying respect for nature and a desire to live in harmony with our surroundings?

A bushcraft course will give you the practical experience necessary to handle many of the problems that could arise in the wilderness. So how about making your next wilderness adventure safer and more enjoyable by attending one?

QUIZ RESULTS

COPING IN THE WILDERNESS
For page 23

If you mostly answered:

a) Well done! You've obviously read and noted the advice given. You should make a sensible hiker.

b) You haven't taken much notice of the advice given and should read it again to make sure you know what to do when hiking in the wilderness.

c) You don't seem to care much about safety and should avoid any adventures in the wild.

SURVIVAL OF THE FITTEST
For page 39

If you mostly answered:

a) You don't seem very fit to survive at all! You should certainly think of going on a survival-training course before you attempt any outdoors adventures.

b) You probably tend to overreact in a crisis, and could do with reading this book again.

c) Well done! You should be fit to survive by making some good choices. You'd be a good companion to have around on a desert island!

KEEPING OUT OF DANGER
For page 31

If you mostly answered:

a) You seemed to have missed the big ideas discussed in this book and should read it again.

b) Well done! You've got the right idea and would probably be good at keeping safe in the wild.

c) You're too worried about money to be thinking about taking a trip to wild places.

⓴ Things To Remember

1 A survival kit is important for any wilderness trip, so make sure yours is fully stocked before heading off.

2 Before leaving, inform another person about your route, destination, and when you expect to be back.

3 A large plastic sheet is a useful item to have at all times, so keep one rolled up in your rucksack.

4 Check weather forecast websites for long-term details before heading out.

5 For anyone lost and alone in the wilderness, remember the acronym STOP: Stop, Think, Observe, Plan.

6 Check trees and rocks to help you find your way. Moss usually grows more on the northern side of rocks, while spider webs tend to be on the south side of trees.

7 If lost, find running water and follow it downstream as it may eventually lead to houses or people.

8 A red sky at dawn often means an approaching low-pressure system is bringing a lot of moisture in the air. It can mean a storm is on its way.

9 If you have no water, tie a small plastic bag over a living plant to collect water droplets for drinking.

10 If you have no food, one way to obtain important nutrients is to eat grubs, worms, and insects.

11 Anyone planning to go on a wilderness expedition should learn how to identify which plants to avoid.

12 When camping, avoid sleeping near water or leaving water in open containers – mosquitoes will be near.

13 Dock leaves can be used as a vegetable and are an excellent source of both vitamin A and protein.

14 Rubbing wild garlic and onion on your skin repels insects and is a natural antiseptic.

15 No toothbrush? You can still clean your teeth using a twig with a chewed end.

16 Three fires lit in a row are an internationally recognised distress signal.

17 In cold conditions, you can lose almost half of your body heat if your head is unprotected – so keep it covered!

18 Do not rely on mobile phones in wild places. They often fail to receive signals in remote areas.

19 If water is scarce in a desert, do not eat. Food requires water for digestion and can use up water you need for cooling.

20 To find your way out of a rainforest, follow one of the many animal trails. These often lead to water or clearings.

Further Information

BOOKS/GUIDES

Essential Bushcraft – A handbook of survival skills, Ray Mears (Hodder & Stoughton, 2003)

Harvesting Nature's Bounty: A Guidebook of Nature Lore, Wild Edible, Medicinal, and Utilitarian Plants and Animals, Kevin F. Duffy (Author House, 2000)

Identifying and Harvesting Edible and Medicinal Plants in Wild (And Not So Wild) Places, Steve Brill and Evelyn Dean Quill (HarperCollins, 1994)

Primitive Living, Self-Sufficiency and Survival Skills: A Field Guide to Primitive Living Skills, Thomas Elpel (Lyons Press, 2004)

WEBSITES

http://www.viven.com.uy/571/eng/Default.asp
Explore the accident in the Andes that occurred in 1972.

http://www.redcross.org.uk/TLC.asp?id=75758
First aid training, products, and tips from the British Red Cross.

http://www.theaward.org/youth/flash.html
Try for one of three Duke of Edinburgh awards you can achieve during your spare time, for anyone aged 14–25.

http://travel.howstuffworks.com/survival.htm
Read about true survival stories.

http://www.hunter-ed.com/mi/course/ch8_water.htm
Learn how to make a solar still to collect water.

http://www.raymears.com/Bushcraft_Courses/Junior/
Junior survival courses for adventurous youngsters.

http://www.scouts.org.uk/
Be prepared for adventures and activities designed for young people aged 6–25.

http://weather.yahoo.com/
Check the weather before you go.

http://www.wilderness-survival-skills.com/wilderness-survival-books.html
Books you can buy to learn more about wilderness survival.

http://www.wilderness-survival-skills.com/index.html
Discover all kinds of survival advice.

**http://www.woodlandsurvivalcrafts.com/survival-courses/
schools-youth.php**
Programmes for young people in search of a wilderness adventure.

Glossary

allergic having an unpleasant reaction (such as sneezing, itching, or rashes) to substances

antibiotics medicines that fight infection and diseased tissue

antiseptic substance that prevents the growth of germs that cause disease or decay

antivenom biological product used in the treatment of venomous bites or stings

avalanche mass of snow, ice, and rocks falling rapidly down a mountainside

bear-proof container hard-sided, portable container for storing food, approved as bear-resistant. Throughout many parts of bear country in the United States it is illegal not to store food properly.

camouflaged hidden or disguised by blending in with one's surroundings

carbohydrates mainly sugars and starches that provide a major energy source in the diet

charred scorched and changing to charcoal or carbon by heating

dehydration to lose water or body fluids, which can lead to serious illness

EPIRB Emergency Position Indicating Radio Beacon

fatal causing death

habitat place or environment where a plant or animal usually lives

hypothermia reduction of the body temperature to a seriously low level

improvise to make or invent from what is conveniently at hand without time to plan carefully

kindling small twigs used for lighting fires

larvae young wormlike form (such as a grub or caterpillar) that hatches from insect eggs

malaria disease caused by mosquitoes. Malaria can be fatal.

marooned left isolated and helpless

nutrients substances that provide nourishment for life and growth

parasites living things that survive in, or on, another living thing

phonetic sounds used in speech

porous able to absorb moisture through tiny holes

predators animals that live by killing and eating other animals

proteins essential nutrient for healthy bodies, supplied by foods such as meat, milk, eggs, nuts, or beans

spindle slender, round rod or stick that can be twisted at speed by hand

summit highest point of a hill or a mountain

tinder any dry material that ignites with a few sparks

toxic poisonous

track follow a trail left by someone or something

transpire give off water vapour through leaves of plants

wilderness area where few people live that is not used for farming and is mostly in its natural state

Index